GAREL MASTER CLASS

The other Agent isn't responding
Finance is dropping the ball
Your potential clients won't commit
Contract difficulties
Can't close a deal......

Feeling a little overwhelmed?

Garel Master's Class

Text Copyright Donna Garel 2024

All rights reserved. No part of this book may be reproduced or transmitted in any form or by any means, electronic or mechanical, including photocopying, recording, or by an information storage and retrieval system - except by a reviewer who may quote brief passages in a review to be printed in a magazine or newspaper - without permission in writing from the publisher.

B/W Illustrations by John Montgomery

ISBN 978-1-304-25731-4
Imprint: Lulu.com

Garel Master's Class

Introduction..5
Mastering Your Business..5
    Your Why...5
    Your Database..9
    Time Management..10
    Basic Assumptions...11
    Farming..12
    Using Social Media Efficiently..18
        Social Media...18
        Your social media presence..18
        Designing your Website...20
        How to be seen: SEO's (Search Engine Optimization)...26
        How to set up your Google Business Listing.................27
        Social Media Platforms and Strategies.........................27
       29

Where the Pedal hits the Medal..31
    The Realtor Box - "The Lifesaver Box"...............................32
    Buyers..34
        Find and Win Buyers..34
        Buyer: Make and Receive Offers..................................38
        Buyer: Negotiate, Deal, Contract to Close....................55
    Sellers...63
        Seller Leads..63
        Seller Appointments..65
        Seller: Marketing Your Listing.......................................69
        Seller: Receive Offers...78
        Seller: Negotiate Deal...87
    Leases..93
        Why Lease?..93
        What To Expect When Applying for a Property Lease...95
        Leasing: Finding & Showing homes; Overcoming Challenges......97
        Leasing Client Approved: Now What?.........................102
        Submitting an Application for a Lease.........................105

Garel Master's Class

Open Houses 107
    Tips for a Successful Open House 107
    Navigating the Open House Contract 108
    Open House note for Buyers and Sellers 110
    Prologue 114

Garel Master's Class

Garel Master Class
Master your business
    Gain lasting clients
        Get your tools for success
                and know how to utilize them

Garel Master's Class

Introduction

Mastering Your Business

Your Why

Your Why should answer: "Why are you doing this?"
Take some time and write your answer:

_____

_____

_____

_____

_____

_____

_____

Garel Master's Class

Why do you want to succeed at this?

_____

_____

_____

_____

_____

_____

_____

_____

Garel Master's Class

Why is it important to you?

_____

_____

_____

_____

_____

_____

_____

Now, ask yourself why you gave the answers above. For instance, if you answered, "To add $50,000 to our family income" In the space below, answer why you want to add $50,000 to your family income.

Why?

_____

_____

_____

_____

Garel Master's Class

One more time. Why is your answer above important to you?

_____

_____

_____

_____

Do you see any words recurring in your answers? Maybe you see the phrase "quality of life" recurring or maybe you find the word "best" recurring

Use your new insights from your three answers and your recurring themes to restructure and rewrite your Big WHY:

_____

_____

_____

_____

_____

_____

Garel Master's Class

Your Database

I need to briefly address the importance of your database. Get in the Green!

One vital key to your success is to keep your database updated and accurate. Be sure all your key categories are in the green. My database will show me the percentage of phone numbers, emails, neighborhoods and addresses I have in my contacts database. Having one of these key areas in red is not conducive to our success. Make sure you are in the green in all of them!

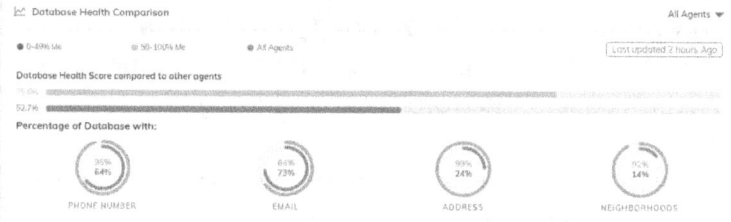

Garel Master's Class

Time Management

Managing your time is critical and can make or break your day. You want to schedule your time very deliberately. Here's an example and a place to begin making notes for your own schedule.

7:00-8:00 AM Wake up, Exercise, Nutrition	Use this time to fuel your body and energize yourself for the busy day ahead!
8:00 - 9:00 AM Morning Power Hour	Set yourself up to be in a peak mental state – this is crucial to reaching your goals. It may be: prayer, meditation, visualization, affirmations, etc
9:00 – 10:00 AM Prep + Review	Sit down with your calendar, update your time blocks if your schedule has changed. Go over your objectives and outcomes for the day. Review the hot sheets to keep your finger on the pulse of the market. Do some role playing to enhance your negotiation skills, your conversion notess or your objection handlers. You can review your Ignite notes
10:00 - 11:30 AM Appointment Setting	No distractions, just 90 minutes straight of prospecting and appointment setting (DO NOT SKIP THIS!)
11:30 – 12:00 PM Social Media	Post and answer your social media, plan ads, campaigns, live videos etc.

Garel Master's Class

Record Your Mornings:

Day/Date	Time Activity

Basic Assumptions

For the purpose and scope of this book, I'm assuming you already know the importance of practicing and knowing what you will say in your conversations.. You are already calling the contacts in your database daily to generate leads and sales. Together now we'll look into how to catapult your business from there!

Garel Master's Class

Farming

Have you ever considered Farming? Farming is a great way to establish a territory and make new contacts!

We will divide Farming into three sections:

> What you need to HAVE
>
> What you need to DECIDE
>
> What you need to DO

I've boiled down all the information in each section into five succinct, digestible, and most importantly readable and "DOABLE" bites.

Important: I suggest that you one document at a time and complete each step before moving on to the next.

Garel Master's Class

You can work on a step a day, a category a day, or see how much you can finish in a week. It's all up to you according to the timetable and goals of your business. Let's begin!

5 Things you need to Have
There are five major things you need to have and utilize before you can be successful at farming an area.

1. **S**ocial Media accounts
2. **C**ards
3. **L**ead Tracker: KW Command to track your leads
4. **P**rofessional Website
5. **D**oor Hangers

You can remember these categories by this acronym:
Success: **C**lients **L**ove **P**rofessionalism & **D**ependability

Professionalism, consistency and dependability should be the backbone of everything you do. If you are not professional and consistent, you will not be successful.

Garel Master's Class

5 Things you need to Decide:

- Research your chosen demographic.

You can't be effective in helping a chosen demographic unless you understand their desires and their needs. This knowledge is critical to finding the right properties for your clients. For instance, if your demographic is retirees, you might find out that in your area, they want to downsize and have a quiet place to live. You would not then show them a large property in the midst of a noisy, bustling area. Make sure neighbors see your sign in area yards. The neighbors will begin to consider you an authority and know you have the inside track.

- What business will you partner with?

Why would you want to take the time to partner with a local business? Local businesses from grocery stores and restaurants to medical offices offer great opportunities because of the established connections they have with residents. They have connections with the locals that you do not. They are meeting the needs of the neighborhood daily and are known and trusted. When you partner with a local business, some of the confidence that the neighborhood has in the business will also be attributed to you. You will also get repeat exposure. You can get access to the names of businesses through the local Chamber of Commerce

- Decide on a property specialization.

It is important both to know your buyers and to specialize in the type of properties they need.

Garel Master's Class

If your specialty is retirees, be sure you know the best areas for their desires. Are there extravagant HOA fees while most of your clients have a small fixed income? Is there local transportation available? Delivery services? Where are the nearest grocery stores and pharmacies? What amenities does each community offer? This knowledge will allow you to determine an effective pricing strategy.

- Will you invest in helps like a scheduling program for social media or Parkbench to be consistent in outreach and gathering statistics

Scheduling programs for social media post to all your accounts for you. You can preschedule them to post at the most popular times for engagement. So, if 10am is the best time to post on Facebook, LinkedIn and Instagram on a particular day, how will you do that if you are in the middle of showing a property or in a meeting? A scheduling program allows you to sit down at a time that is convenient for you and schedule posts to go to all your social media platforms. Socialpilot and Hootsuite are two popular choices. There are also sites like Parkbench which, for a not so nominal fee will deliver "an interactive and content-rich website for their neighborhood that automatically updates every day with local events, news and deals".

- Will you pay for ads on social media?

Facebook ads are a popular and efficient way to reach people that you have not yet met in person. In seconds, people can see your face, your message and what you have to offer.

Garel Master's Class

Facebook particularly allows you the ability to hone in on the specific audience you want to reach - ie your farming area. Research the ways you can use ads and see if, for your target group, the cost to benefit would be beneficial.

5 Things you Have to Do
- Attend events

Attending events is a great way to "billboard yourself" and get your face in front of the community. You can meet people one on one, establish relationships, make contacts, hand out business cards, gain credibility and you don't even have to plan it - just show up! And, like everything we do, show up consistently. Look for events from neighborhood get togethers in a park to events hosted by local businesses.

- Host events

Hosting events is another important way to establish yourself as an authority in your farming community. It shows that you care enough to put time and energy organizing an event to add value to their lives. The more consistent you are in hosting, the greater your return on investment.

- Sponsor local sports

When do Real Estate sales rise? Did you know that historically in the spring properties sell almost 20% faster? When you sponsor a team, your logo and name can be printed on team uniforms. The players are like walking billboards for you - all. season. long. You can

Garel Master's Class

also print posters and banners that include your head shot, and contact details. Set them up around the event during games.

- Partner with local businesses

Once you've decided *what* business you want to partner with, you need to decide on *how* you will partner with them. I've been in some local restaurants or tea shops that have a TV that you can share advertisements with. You can use slides, make a personal video, or even create an ad that is similar to what is seen on cable. Use it to introduce yourself, your services and contact details. Leave your card and other marketing material in a place that will be seen. If you pin your card on a corkboard with hundreds of other cards, you just wasted a card. If you partner with a business to leave a stack of cards by their register, now you have created an opportunity!

- Be consistent

I've been saying it and now I'm putting it in its own category. Why? It will make or break you. Be consistent in all you do. Be consistent in your use of social media, websites, events, mailers, door hangers, pop bys, phone calls and emails. It should go without saying that once you decide on an area or genre of clientele, do not change it. Be constant and consistent. Don't run after the next shiny, promising area when you have begun to put roots into a different one. If you continue to pull up roots before the plant is grown, your business will not succeed. Keep your name, your face and your brand in front of the people you want to reach. People will begin to expect you to be a part of their community and it will negatively impact your reputation to pull up roots prematurely.

Garel Master's Class

Using Social Media Efficiently

Social Media

Your social media presence

It is important to have a strong social media presence on the most popular platforms. Your potential customers need to easily find you on their favorite social media sites. In 2020, the most popular social media sites were Facebook, Instagram, Youtube and Twitter. I personally also post to my LinkedIn account, as it gives me access to a professional clientele. To make best use for your time, using Hootsuite or another scheduler, post on social media accounts, Facebook, LinkedIn, Instagram and Twitter at 10am and 6pm Monday-Friday. You can choose to make one or more of the days themed or catchy, like "Throwback Thursday" where you show houses or decor back in the day, or "Fun Friday" where you post something fun, or funny. You want to post for engagement. You want to establish contact, and repeated contact breeds relationships. So ask questions, do polls, offer giveaways. Whatever it takes to engage them! A general rule for posting is 80-90% non business related content and 10-20% business related posts. Do not only post your listings! You will lose followers quickly.

Garel Master's Class

Some sources to pull from can include:

- https://texashillcountry.com
- www.houzz.com
- austin.culturemap.com
- www.housingwire.com

If the local links don't apply to you, search for some local online publications. You'll probably find more than you think. They can have great content and you are helping a small business by directing people to their pages.

Garel Master's Class

Designing your Website

Things to keep in mind when designing your website: There are four key factors to keep in mind when you create your website.

1. Conveying your message/brand immediately
2. Branding a photo
3. Easy ways to contact you
4. Providing other resources

Let's dig in.
You'll want to design your website so when people visit, you can convey the most important information and get their attention in the first 10 seconds.

Let's take a look at my website. The first thing they will see is my branded picture of me (we'll get to that in a minute) as well as an information button.

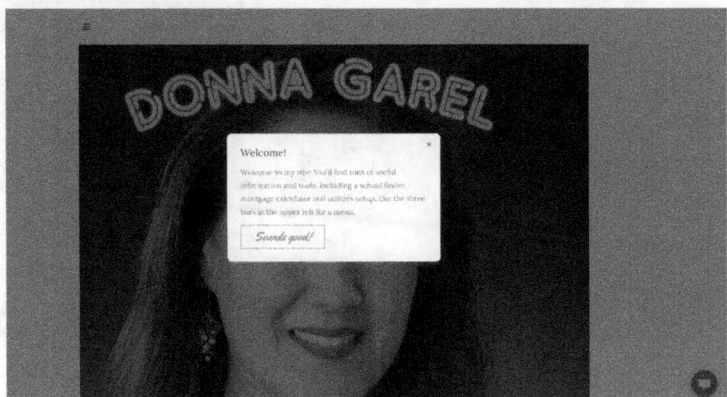

Garel Master's Class

In the first few seconds, I relayed a lot of information all at once. They have a face to put near my name. They know something about my character and how I operate. They see that there are reviews available to read if they scroll down. They see that they can schedule an appointment. And, a pop up when they first come to my website advises them there are also many tools they can access to help them.

Garel Master's Class

Let's talk about branding your headshot. What is it and why should you do it?

Every agent (I hope) has a professional headshot. What makes you stand out? Branding your photo! What information do you want to convey about your business or character? People are visual, and we connect with faces. A branded headshot can, at times, be more effective than a business card.

Let's take a look at mine:

Garel Master's Class

Use fonts and colors that reinforce your message. My photo conveys that I am loved because I have satisfied customers.

When you create your brand, do not attach it to your company because if you change companies, all you have built in your brand is tied to a company you are no longer with. It makes you appear inconsistent or unstable. Your brand is YOU, not your company.
How will you create your brand?

It should be easy for existing and potential clients to get in touch with you through your website. Be sure you have ways to contact you in multiple places on your site that are easy and quick to find.

Another tool that will set you apart from competition is to have tools your customers can use on your website. Do they need a school search? Mortgage calculator?

Garel Master's Class

Let's take a look at some tools I offer:

If we use a wide angle lens to zoom out on the top of the first page on my website, you'll see the menu on the upper left and then all the information available to them instantly:

Garel Master's Class

Notice how my social media is listed here as well. They can also find my social media at the bottom of my page along with a map to my location.

Garel Master's Class

How to be seen: SEO's (Search Engine Optimization)

What is Search Engine Optimization and why should you spend time on it? Search engine optimization (SEO) is the process of optimizing your online content so that a search engine will likely show you as a top result for searches of certain keywords. When it comes to SEO, there are three entities. We have the search engine, the searcher and you. When people search for your name or your job, or the area in which you have most of your listings, you want the search engine (usually Google) to show *you* as a top result. Think about what keywords you want to be number one in results. If your name is "Joe Smith" and you are a realtor in NYC, you might want to be in the top listings when people search for

Jane Doe
Jane Doe Realtor
Realtor TX
Realtor, Texas
Joe Smith, TX
Joe Smith, Texas
Joe Smith, Real Estate
Real Estate, Texas

And so on. As you build your website and fill in your information for search engines, like your google business page and your branded website, be sure to embed at least one of these keywords or phrases on each page.

Garel Master's Class

How to set up your Google Business Listing

1. Access your Google business login or, if you don't have one, create a new Google Account
2. Go to Google.com/business and click <Manage Now>
3. Fill in the information on the Google business page. Be sure to have your address, hours, website information and lots of photos!
4. You will need to choose your business category. This is critical as it influences what searches you appear in.
5. Finally, you will need to verify your business with Google and complete your Google My Business Verification.

Social Media Platforms and Strategies

To run efficiently and effectively on social media means having a plan and a scheduler.

Commanding a well thought out social marketing strategy is crucial to your business. Posts should be well organized, share informative or engaging content. Your post content needs to be driven by your marketing and business plan. This is a tangible and measurable way to help you achieve your goal. You will need to establish a schedule and plan to post for each major social network. You can share motivational posts, listings, landing pages with forms, videos and photos. Your content needs to be engaging. 80%-90% of your posts should not be work related. One of the fastest ways to lose followers is to make every post a listing. I will cover five major social media platforms to help get you started.

Garel Master's Class

TikTok!

TikTok may be one of the most important platforms to drive traffic to you. Make at least one 30 second to 1 min video a day. Let them know you the cool person - who just happens to do Real Estate.

Facebook

On Facebook, the more you post, the more Facebook's algorithm will show your posts to others. Let's say you have 100 followers, when you make a post, Facebook does not show that content to all 100 followers. It may be only 15-30 people who will see it. This is determined by the algorithm. The more you post, the more the algorithm thinks you are important and the more people will see your content.

During the week, you'll want to post at least twice a day in the morning and the afternoon or early evening. 9am and 3pm are popular as the kids are in school. You may also want to post around 5pm before people get off work. Most people look through Facebook during work hours! Be sure you don't post more than five times a day. On the weekend posting anytime between noon and 9pm gives good results.

You can create photo albums that contain pictures of your listings and your closings. Be SURE you don't let a closing pass without taking a picture to put on social media. If your clients will give you permission to post a picture with them, even better!

Garel Master's Class

Twitter

Twitter allows posts of only 280 characters, so your posts need to be both succinct and engaging. Because of the fast paced nature of Twitter, tweets have a life of only 18 minutes, so it can be prudent to post more than twice a day on this platform. Weekdays the best times to post on Twitter are between 11am-1pm. The best times on the weekend are around 5pm-6pm.

LinkedIn

LinkedIn can be a powerful lead generating tool, putting your services in front of a professional audience. Establishing your brand on LinkedIn can take some time, but with a mighty payoff. You will want to make sure that your page or company is completely and professionally filled out before posting. The best time to post on LinkedIn is 10-11am weekdays. Wednesday and Thursday are the best times to post. Weekend posts on LinkedIn are often not seen. LinkedIn also has groups targeted to specific interests. You can utilize these for your business by posting relevant content in them.

Instagram

Instagram is a photo based social media network. This is perfect for your listing and closing photos - but be sure to follow the 80-20 rule and have 80% of your content be something that will capture the attention of a wide audience and make them want to continue watching your channel for new content. The best times to post on Instagram during the week is during lunch (11am-1pm) and after dinner (7pm-9pm) and weekends between 11am-12pm.

Garel Master's Class

Scheduling Social Media

You will want to post multiple times a day on all the major social media platforms. While you want to have multiple posts per day on at least four major social platforms, you don't want to spend your day posting. As a matter of fact, social media should be a *small* scheduled block of time in your day. The way to accomplish this is through a scheduling tool.

When we use a scheduling tool for social media, we use our time wisely and proficiently. You will want to schedule posts at certain times of the day. Your followers will come to expect your posts which can help engagement as it helps stack the odds that they will *see* your posts..

For most schedulers, if you want to post every day on a regular basis, there will be a small fee attached.

Ten schedulers you can use as of this writing are:

1. Sendible. Sendible is an all-in-one social media management tool designed to help solopreneurs and agencies manage and amplify their brands. ...
2. AgoraPulse
3. MeetEdgar
4. SmarterQueue
5. Buffer Publish
6. TweetDeck
7. Hootsuite
8. Loomly
9. SEMrush
10. SocialBee

Garel Master's Class

Where the Pedal hits the Medal

Garel Master's Class

The Realtor Box - "The Lifesaver Box"

I advise everyone to put a Realtor box in your car. It will be a lifesaver 10 times over! Here's what my box looks includes...

- Old blanket (used to protect my car from dirt, etc from signs
- Copy Paper Box filled with:
- Roll of Paper Towels
- Roll of Toilet Paper
- Broom/Dust Pan
- Toilet Brush
- Disinfecting Wipes
- Trash Bags
- Rubber and Steel Mallet
- Blue and Green tape
- Hand Sanitizer
- Hand Soap
- Kleenex
- Screwdriver
- Booties
- Gloves
- Golf Ball (this is my level detector for wonky foundations)
- Flashlight
- Gloves
- Masks
- Old plastic container to hold toilet brush, etc
- Tape Measure
- Sticky notes and pen (attached to tape measure)
- My accordion folder with blank documents
- Water Bottles (if I have it, I'll carry a gallon jug of water - used to soften the ground when putting out signs)

Garel Master's Class

As you put your box together, you may find other things that you want to include. These are the items that I have found the most useful in my business and used the most.

Garel Master's Class

Buyers

Find and Win Buyers

A lot of people talk about finding the sellers, which is great, however you also need to be aware that there are also buyers. Think about this, even with a seller- who is going to take that home off of the seller's hand? A buyer. So it is important to know how to work with those buyers!

It is also the case that you tend to find a lot more buyers out there than you will sellers, so that's something you want to keep your eyes and your ears peeled for.

Buyers are all over the place. Think about it. You have somebody out there you're talking with:
one of your co-workers, one of your friends, one of your neighbors, one of your family members, a parent over at your kids soccer team - whatever the case is. You guys are talking about whatever's going on. Let's say, y'all are talking about the soccer game and the kids and the coach and what's happening and how the team's been playing this season, and then the conversation then sparks with, "Hey what do you do?" They discover that you're a Realtor. Next thing you know you have this parent saying, "Oh my gosh, you are?? You know my

Garel Master's Class

friend is really into investment properties and was has been telling me all about the the wonderful extra side income on an investment property. I'd love to start earning with some rentals. You know. it's the end of the season, end of the year and I'm getting ready to get my Christmas bonus from work and so I'd like to take that and use it as a down payment on my first investment property."

You don't have to know everything

You've got people around you that are willing to help. Talk to people that do investing. Learn a little bit. You don't have to know everything.

What did you just hear? You heard a future repeat buyer. You heard an investor. They are looking for your assistance. They're looking for your knowledge. It doesn't matter that you don't have any investment properties and never invested in property. Take a look around. You have co-workers. Think even of independent contractors like co-workers. You've got people around you that are willing to help. Talk to people that do investing. Learn a little bit. You don't have to know everything. Learn a little bit. You'll start to learn more as you go. Talk to this parent a little bit more and find out

Garel Master's Class

what they're looking for. Find out where they want to be. How much do they want to spend? What are they looking to make on a return? Now you have some Information and can put them in touch with the lender. Let the lender run all the numbers for them. Then you can let them know if they want this investment property, it's going to cost this much, and this is what your mortgage payment is going to be with your insurance and taxes and everything. You can advise them that if they want to return a profit, they will need to have the rent set at this price. So, where can we go to get rent at that price with a dollar amount on that price for a house? That's where you come in. You get to go look in the MLS, and you go talk to people and see if anybody has any pocket listings. You may know a great neighborhood that you can then farm and see if anybody has properties that match that person's criteria.

Finding a buyer just takes listening. You could be talking to somebody that is like, "Yeah you know my lease is about up and we're kind of getting tired because the landlord's just not really good. We really need something else." Did you hear that? That's potentially a buyer! How about we have that conversation with that tenant whose lease is about up? You might say, "Hey, instead of leasing again, have you thought about purchasing your own place and not having the landlord issues? Then you're in charge, you get to make those decisions and

Garel Master's Class

don't have to wait for a landlord. It's your own and you can do whatever you want with it."

Look who's out there and listen. Have the conversations and ask the questions. Nurture if needed. Everybody's not pulling the trigger right now.

Look who's out there and listen. Have the conversations and ask the questions. Nurture if needed. Everybody's not pulling the trigger right now. You're going to have some that are going to pull the trigger in six months. I've had some that didn't pull the trigger for three years. I nurtured them for three years to have them eventually close a deal and it was a very nice deal!

So think about it. Go out there and see who you can find. Keep those leads. You're keeping those people because you're going to continue to nurture them. Ask them the questions: "How can I help? What can I offer you? How can I help get you to your end goal?" You are the resource, so be that resource they'll remember. They will think of you as their own Agent and resource. This is how you keep those leads. This is how you convert those potential people into buyer clients.

Garel Master's Class

Buyer: Make and Receive Offers

Let's talk a little bit about negotiations and then about contract to close. I will admit negotiations is my happy place! I really enjoy that it's a phase of that transaction in which you really want to make all parties feel like it's a win-win. I have received multiple comments from other agents on the other side of deals that I have negotiated that said they really appreciated working with me because I made it feel like a win-win for both parties.

Your goal is not to come in with the negotiations and be a really hard, gruff negotiator so that the other side doesn't like you. If you do that, you're going to hit somebody like me on the other side and I'm going to dig my heels into the ground and we're done. When negotiation starts to turn into a point of principle for one party, it's a stopping point and you have hit a boulder. Make it a win-win. You will ask. You will give. The other side will respond, and they will give and ask, and we come together collaboratively and agree to something that both parties mutually will accept.

Garel Master's Class

Understand when you are actually under Contract.

When you get a contract, you have both parties have signed and it's been executed. I'm talking about a contract here in Texas. In another state it may work a little bit differently, however in Texas once both parties have signed and the contract has been executed, that contract goes over to the Title Company and to the lender. The Title Company is collecting earnest and option money. They will receive that contract and now we are fully under contract.

When that happens, we're ready to continue to the next phase. The first full day after the execution, (meaning all parties have signed and money may or may not have been turned over to title) is the first full day after that date is the start of the option period here in Texas.

Therefore, it's imperative that the buyers get an inspector as quickly as possible out to the property to take a look at it. You don't want to waste any of that option period waiting for an inspector to come out and then have him come out the second to the last day of your option period. Then you have no time to negotiate. Get that inspector out as quickly as possible.

Agents, it is imperative that you have your tribe around you. Your trusted tribe are your lenders, your inspectors, your appraisers and anybody else that you need. Have that trusted tribe because your inspectors will come out within a day or two for you because you're part of the trusted tribe. So be sure you have those and you give those options over to your buyers so they can select and pick one. Let your buyers know to pick an inspector and get it scheduled ASAP. If you can have that inspector come out today, let's get that inspector out today! Inspector goes out and does the inspection, you get the inspection report back usually that evening or the next day after the inspection depending on what the scheduling is like. Look through the report, have your clients look through that report and identify things that need to be fixed.

There's going to be some stuff in there. The inspector noticed that there is a broken window. That's kind of a big thing. You might say, "I'd like that window fixed before we closed." Or, "There's a missing door - we need a door put on there." Maybe the sink doesn't drain. These are the kind of issues to address when you are looking at that inspection report.

Garel Master's Class

When you read about the little piddly stuff like, "oh there's a little scuff on the back of the door where the lock went on." Or, " The door hit it and it dented it. There's a couple of holes in the wall because they had pictures there and they pulled the nails out. Around the window we need a little bit of caulking..." When you look and read that inspection report, take a look at it and look for things that feel good to ask for. Either money or repairs for those items.

Pretend that report is on your house and you were the seller. Pretend the buyer's gonna come in and be like, "Oh you know so there's a little bit of caulking that needs to happen over there on the kitchen counter and so we want you guys to caulk the whole kitchen. There's a scuff mark behind the door so we need the whole house painted."

How do you feel? Not very good. Are you calling a bluff, saying, "Do you want this house or not?" That's regular wear and tear and you're going to scuff that wall moving your stuff in.

If the buyers come back per that report and notice that the electricity is not working in one of the bedrooms at all and they ask for that to be fixed, how do you feel about that? Electricity seems important. We need to have the plugs working. We need to have the light

Garel Master's Class

switches working. We need to have the electricity working in that room because it currently is not usable. So, what are you going to ask for? What are you going to recommend? Things that feel good.

Explain it that way to your clients because your clients don't understand. They see the inspection report. It is 60 pages long and it is scary. They're thinking "Oh my. There's everything wrong with this house!" No no. Everything's not wrong with the house. There's just various things that are maintenance and then there's other things that could be big things. Weed through these items. Have your clients look through that report. Have them identify the things that they are really concerned about. Come together and ask them for their list. Take note of what they have on their list and walk through it. You might reply, "Oh yeah, I noticed that broken window too. We're gonna definitely ask for that. We did notice that the seal of the toilet in the master bathroom is broken and has been leaking. We can see that there's rotted baseboards up underneath there and some potential for some mold damage -so we're going to ask them to fix that.

Oh, the caulking around the counters in the kitchen? If the buyer was asking you about that caulking, would you be like you think, "Just go to the store and buy a two dollar bottle of caulk and caulk the darn thing?"

Garel Master's Class

So let's take a look at the big items. Let's look at the stuff that feels good. Ask for the stuff that if somebody was asking you to either pay to have somebody come in and fix it or fix it for them it feels good.

After this, you have a final list from that inspection report. If you are unsure of how much to ask for if your client wants to ask for money, contact one of your tribe. Talk to your handyman. Talk to your contractor. Call the inspector and ask the inspector what they feel these things would cost to repair. Ask the inspector what the big things are.

Once you have the big things identified, then you and your client can decide what to do. Decide what you want fixed and I highly recommend asking for the money versus the repairs, because then your client gets to get who they want to do the repairs like Uncle Bob who is not licensed or anything.

I want it fixed properly, so I recommend asking for the money. In certain situations there may be somebody coming in and do the fixes I understand that can happen.

In your negotiations, you will then put together your amendment for either. When asking for repairs, be very specific. For instance, "I need a licensed certified HVAC

specialist to come in and service the HVAC system with a receipt provided one week prior to closing.
Be very specific if there is something else that needs to be done. If you leave anything loose for interpretation, it *will* be interpreted, and it may not be interpreted how you think it should be interpreted.

If you're asking for money, and you've talked with the inspector, then you've talked with trades that come in and help you identify that you may have: a roofer that comes out and takes a look at it and gives you a quote on what repairs need to be done on the roof. You may have a structural engineer that comes in or a plumber to take a look at the leaky faucet.

Whoever you have come in, you've got quotes from them. Those are awesome because that's hard documentation on what the repairs would cost. You can add all of those up together now and can take that money that you're asking for during the negotiations and you can pull it off the sale price. You can ask for some of that to be used towards closing costs.

Let's talk a little bit about closing costs. If you take money towards closing costs, be sure you've talked with the lender to find out exactly how much the lender will authorize.

Garel Master's Class

Ask the lender how much money they will authorize somebody else to pay for closing costs for your client because if the loan is a small loan they may only allow you three thousand dollars and you may have ten thousand dollars worth of repairs that you're asking for.

If it's a big loan they may authorize that ten thousand dollars. Remember in the state of Texas when you ask for closing cost assistance you only get to use what the lender has approved, so if you've asked for ten thousand dollars and the lender says you can only use three thousand, you have lost. You have left at the table seven thousand dollars that you do not get back. It does not roll into anything else. You have thrown it away. So be sure to talk to the lender and clarify this!

After you have gone through all the negotiations and you've asked for what feels good, the seller has come back and probably had negotiated back and forth a little bit. Everybody's happy. Now we are moving forward to close.

After that negotiations on the buy side, and the agreement on what the negotiation for repairs looks like during that period, the next step really is in the hands of your lender and the Title Company. Therefore, be sure if there's money that you are asking for - whether in what the closing costs are or off the sale price, that you have gotten a copy of that Amendment.

Garel Master's Class

Once it's all signed and executed to the lender and to the Title Company, all parties need a copy. If it's just repairs I don't recommend sending it to the lender because they will want another inspection to come out and verify that those repairs are done, and I was actually told that directly by another lender, so I'm going to caution you on that. Once that negotiation is done everything is in the hands of the lenders and the Title Company, you will communicate back and forth with the lender and the Title Company at least once a week. Twice a week is even better!

Find out how things are going. Can you do anything to help? Do they need anything?

The Title Company is going to be running the background on the house and checking the Title making sure nothing's wrong. They're going to be getting out all of the Title commitments and all of the other stuff on the house checking it and making sure it's clean before they turn it over.

The lender is going to be doing everything they need with your buyer to make sure that your buyers still qualify for that loan, and they all have deadlines. You should start seeing a very various amount of documents coming from the Title Company with the Title commits, the tax certification, and some HOA docs. These are

Garel Master's Class

things that are all on dates, so have your client look them over. Take a look yourself. Is there anything on there that your client is worried about? HOA documents are important because if your client plans to run some sort of business or put a shed or a pool etc., that they're wanting to put in their house when they buy it, and they learn through those HOA documents that they can't do it, then there's a way to back out if you've put that notice in the contract.

So there's a lot of back-outs for the buyers. You just have to make sure you manage everything and you don't wait to get those documents reviewed.

Don't do extra work! You have a team of specialists!

If they have questions, call the Title Company. Call your Escrow Agent. Sit down with your Escrow Agent and walk through it. You do not have to be the expert on

Garel Master's Class

reading those documents! That's what your Escrow Agent is for. That's why they're getting paid. They're getting paid to help explain all of that. If there's an issue with the lender call the lender find out what's going on. Ask them, "How can we resolve this? What do we need to do?" It could be as simple as having somebody else sign on something, or it could be super super complicated. Ask. Those experts are there to help get through the situation.

As you start to get close to the end and you've been communicating with Title and the lender, the lender will finally give you the clear to close.

 We've passed everything through underwriting and we are approving the loan. You have that clear to close in Texas. I'm not sure about any of the other states, however in Texas the lender has 72 hours to disclose those final numbers before closing.

Talk with your clients if your state has something similar. Be sure you talk with your clients about that when you get that email from the lender open it immediately and click that you have received it. Once you click <acknowledge> it starts that clock that's 72 hours.

Garel Master's Class

They can't just send it to you. They have to send it to you and you have to open it.

Look for that email, open it up and get that clock ticking!

Now when you talk with the Title Company, make sure you have everything you need. Have you gotten documents from the lender yet? Can I see that final settlement statement? Review the numbers. Take a look through your files. Is the sales price correct? Are they getting a refund back for the earnest and the option money? Did the Title Company remember to put that home warranty that you requested the seller to purchase on there? Are your commissions correct? Take a look at all of that and when you have all of that put together, and the lender's done what they need to do, the Title Company has sent you out that closing document and you looked at all the numbers and it looks good, and they are ready to go...... be sure to let the Title company know it is time to book the closing!

Garel Master's Class

Talk to your clients. Ask, "When do you want that closing done?" Get it scheduled for them. It's still your job to do what you can for them. They should feel like you were right there making this super easy for them. Both the negotiations and transaction need to be a win-win. You want your clients coming back and referring you to everybody they know, so make it super smooth and easy for them.

Let's look at critical step some Agents miss

You've got your closing scheduled. You've got the final document and you know how much money that client needs to wire to the Title Company for closing. You know that they need to have it wired before they go sit down at the closing table because ideally the Title at the Escrow Agent comes into the office with the documents ready to sign and says, "We have received your wire. The number is correct."

I'm gonna get on a soapbox right now. I have a financial background, and this is a very touchy subject. This holds true for all states, all countries -anywhere.

Garel Master's Class

Once you get that final number that your client needs to wire to the Title Company for closing, realize it's usually a relatively large number, especially with a conventional loan or somebody that's looking to put some money down to reduce what their loan is. This is one of the biggest checks that your client will ever write. Yes it's a wire I know - yet I'm still looking at it as being a check because it's money that's coming out of their account. It's a big amount of money, and if that money is lost that's detrimental to them. Therefore, before that closing, after you have scheduled the time for closing and you are about to call your client and have them start setting up that wire transfer with their bank and confirming the number - you will verbally confirm wiring instructions with the Title Company. If the Title Company won't send you wiring instructions, they have sent it to your client and your client will send it over to you.

I will print out wiring instructions. I will instruct my client to print out wire instructions so they will have a hard copy. On that copy I will have them write the dollar amount that needs to be wired. They will write that on that piece of paper. I will call the Title Company and I will confirm the wiring instructions based on what I have just printed out, and if there are any errors in there we will fix that and I will write it on this sheet. Then I will let my client know to update it on their sheet, and they will take that sheet to the bank with them and hand it to the teller that is doing that wire transfer, so that that information is correct.

I have a financial background and I don't have trust in some of the electronics that somebody has not tampered with something. If I have not verbally confirmed it, and the Title Company is not calling me to confirm, that I make that phone call. I confirm that I'm calling them on the same number that I have been calling them on this whole time and talking to them.

Please, this is one step I encourage you to really hold true and fast. I have seen moments where sixty thousand dollars was wired to a fraudulent account. Boom! Once that wire leaves, the chances of you getting that money back, your client getting that money back, is next to nil.

Again, that can mean they don't get the house. They don't have the money. What are they doing now? They're freaking out because they have lost all this money and they have no money left in the bank to complete the next steps.

Please, please, please, please, please, be adamant about this!

Garel Master's Class

So now, you've confirmed wiring instructions. We've got the closing schedule. We've contacted our client about how to do the wire. They've sent the pay. They've taken the paperwork to the bank with them. The wire is done, everything's good. You meet your clients there for the closing.

Be sure they bring a check. If they have it just in case there's any money that's being returned. Make sure they have a form of ID. In some states it may be more than a driver's license.

Prior to closing be sure you take your clients back over to the house and have that final walk through. Iin Texas they actually have that walk through document that they can note anything that hasn't been fixed and they can sign so that we can send it over to the other party and make sure that they understand that things haven't been finished. Depending on what they are, we may push closing out. Be sure you go and take a look. If your clients are not here, you need to go look for your clients. It's imperative to go and take a look and make sure everything is good to go.

They go to the closing. You're going to be there. Let the Escrow Agent do their thing and you're there to support and make sure everything's running smoothly. If there are any questions your clients have, this is when you have those conversations.

Garel Master's Class

So, you were there from the beginning, the negotiations all the way to the end when they actually signed the paperwork. Find out exactly when they get to have the keys. Your client signs at the table. They've got keys. The money has been wired over the lender.
Happy day! That's payday for you!

I know there are a lot of steps, however each step is important to guide your client through the whole process.

Garel Master's Class

Buyer: Negotiate, Deal, Contract to Close

You have clients. You have shown them a number of homes, or maybe one home and they love the house. This is a house they want to put the offer in on. Awesome!

First of all be sure as you're showing a buyer a home especially if it is a planned showing, that you have you have MLS information on that home so that when you pop into the house and they ask, "How many square feet is it?" you can answer, "It's 2037 square feet."

"How many bedrooms?" "It's got four bedrooms." You have all the information on there. You know exactly what's going on. For instance you may be able to say, "It looks like the seller right here is offering a buy down. They're offering five thousand dollars towards a buydown on your loan." You need that information for yourself so when you go in and you show that property!

On the back of the form that has the information on the property, I will do a quick market analysis. I'm not going to run a full-blown CMA, however I am going to search up some active some pendings and some closed within 0 to 90 days around that home and get some information on that so that I can take a look at that really quickly and identify where I feel that house should be

Garel Master's Class

priced. Now that we've had a chance to see it and see what kind of condition it's in, your clients may get starry-eyed in this house. The wife is giddy, she is giggling and the kids are already picking their rooms out. The husband has gone nuts over the three-car garage where the third Bay is set up as a woodworking shop. This is their dream home. I don't like to use that word, however in their eyes this is their dream home.

In this scenario, you know because when you booked the showing you knew that there were three showings in front of you that you were not able to get an earlier slot and you know that there's two more showings after you. Does that give you a sign people liked the pictures? People liked the location. Maybe they liked the price. Maybe it was the features of the home. There's interest in that home. You are not the only one starry-eyed. They want the house.

First question they ask after they say, "We love it! We want it!" is, "What should we offer on this house?" Don't give them the list price. Take a look at your paper and you can say right now, "It looks like they've got this home listed at 450,000 and according to comps in the area this home based on the condition is in great condition and we have a couple of homes over here on this list that are in similar condition and that one over there is really bad condition..." You start giving them what you feel that range should be. I like to give a range and I

Garel Master's Class

want them to tell me what they're going to bring for that price. Then they'll give you the price. You tell them, "Based on these numbers, right here the actual market value on the house really should be 455, so they've priced this a little bit below Market. Really based on the condition or maybe their agent didn't know - so it's $5,000 below market value, and because of everything that's happened here, I really feel that this house is valued anywhere between that 455 to about 465. Where would you like to come in on an offer price?"

If you ask your buyers, they may say they want 465. They may say they want 450.

Ask them the next question, "Okay so you guys said that you'd like to come in at 450. At the list price. What is your walk away price? What do I mean by that? I mean the price that when you go to bed tonight and discover that you did not win the offer on this home you will sleep fine. You will not have restless sleep because you didn't offer one dollar more. What is that price? That's not the price that I'm going to draft up that offer at. That's just the price that I know I can negotiate to. Are you okay if I need to negotiate up to that dollar amount?"

If I learn that there's multiple offers on this property and I get an idea of where those multiple offers are at, ask them if they will allow you to negotiate. I always ask them before because they're going to have to sign the

Garel Master's Class

changes anyways and I'll talk with them about it, however I want them to feel like I'm there representing them and I will only use that price if needed. My job is to get them the house, so I need to know what their tolerances are.

Now we have the price. The next imperative thing to do is to call the agent. I cannot stress this enough. A lot of the newer agents do not like picking up the telephone. We are a people business. People talk. We've got to talk and we've got to ask the questions. If we don't ask the questions we don't know the answers. Call the agent up, "Hey just showed your listing and my clients love the house. They've asked me to bring an offer in. Do you mind if I ask you a few questions about the house?"

As you listen you may find out the clients are going to need a lease back. You may find there's some things here that could potentially win the deal in a multiple offer situation. You can ask when their clients need to close by or when would they like to close. Do they want a quick close? Do they want a little bit longer closing time? You may find they are willing to leave the refrigerator in the washer and dryer. You can confirm things like, "I see on here on the MLS that it says they're included I just want to confirm that that's okay." Find out if there is a preferred Title Company. Are there any other offers on the table? What's their deadline?

Garel Master's Class

Find some information out and get the feel because if you're bringing an offer today and they say we're not going to look at any offers for 14 days, do you really need to bring an offer today? Knowing that now they've got something in hand and they're going to be telling everybody else that they have got one at full price right now so if you want the house you got to raise it and they have 14 days to find somebody that's willing to pay more.

I don't trust that even if an agent has told me that they're going to come back and allow us to do highest and best with every offer that's there that they will follow through. I've had that experience where agents have said yes we're going to have the highest and best and they don't ever do it. They just get an offer and they take it and they've left me out so I have no ability to go back and negotiate more for my clients. So once you've got the information and take a look depending on the situation, maybe your clients have to sell their house before they can buy. Find out if the seller will take a contingency. Find out the things you need to know so that you know how to go back to your clients and talk. Let them know what's going on, what you've discovered and it will help you know how to write up the offer.

Take the information and go back to your clients. Let them know what you have found out and ask them how

Garel Master's Class

they want to proceed. Find out where they want to come in on the offer and how much they are putting down.

Get information and start drafting that up. Get that over to them to sign, Let them know if they are cutting off offers that day. Make sure your clients know that you are going to draft this up right now and it's imperative that you guys get this signed quickly so that you can get it back within the time period. Let them know if they're having a hard cut off at five o'clock tonight that you don't want to miss.

Be sure your clients have that pre-qualification or pre-approval from the lender. You should have already had that before you even started taking them out to show properties.

Let the lender know that you guys are putting an offer in. A lot of lenders will call the listing agent and say, "My clients are well qualified and we are ready to get moving on this loan and get this deal closed." It's imperative that the lender is in the loop. Now once all of that's done, there may be some more negotiations. It could be that if it's a multiple offer situation and you have submitted your offer and you've talked with the agent a little bit about what's going on, that the sellers may have said,

Garel Master's Class

"You know we really like these people and their offer is really close to another offer that we like the offer better than their offer but we really like these people."

This could happen because I shared a little bit of information about my clients to get the deal. Those sellers may come back and say, "If you can raise your price from 450 to 455- everything else constant, we will take your offer." Great. It may play out like this: "That's wonderful, let me call my clients real quickly. I'll call you right back." Call your clients and let them know they are in a multiple offer situation. The seller said, "If you can go up to 455 they'll take your offer and everything else is constant." I might say, "You good to go? ... Great, I'm going to send you the paperwork real quick to initial that change. Sign it now. I'm going to call the agent back telling them that I'm getting that signed right now and getting it over." Call the agent and say, "My clients accept. I am getting it signed right now and I will send it to you in just a moment." Timing is of the essence here. We don't want somebody else coming in middle of those conversations and getting things signed with the $550,000 offer out of the blue because if the sellers haven't signed, the buyers haven't signed and it hasn't been executed, when another thing comes through they can turn around and say they got an offer they preferred - sorry.

Garel Master's Class

Timing is of the essence and then once you've got everything under contract and everything is signed, executed and the documents go to the lender. Then the documents go to the Title Company. The Title Company will collect Earnest and option money from your clients and they will receive that contract you were fully under, and you're under contract!

Garel Master's Class

Sellers

Seller Leads

You know listings are the life of the business. With listings all other business comes. This is how you find your leases. This is how you find your landlords. This is how you find your buyers. You want to lead with listings. So, how do you find those listings well? Think about it. As you're having those conversations out there which you should be having every day, you're going to listen to see if anybody is possibly interested in a new area. They'll talk about buying all day long. You have to interpret that conversation and what they've said about buying with a reply like, "Oh, you're interested in this new neighborhood that's coming up over here." or "You guys want to move over here to get a bigger house. Are you going to sell your house or are you going to keep it? What are your plans for your current house? Find out and ask the questions because they haven't thought about that. They've thought about where they want and what they want to buy but they haven't thought about what the process is, and what they need to do. Ask the questions.

Take a look in your neighborhood. You may have a house that is maybe not looking so great. You know it's a rental. It is not really that well taken care of. Maybe

Garel Master's Class

there's people in and out. There's something going on with that house. Your Spidey senses are going off. Take a look in the tax records and find out who the owner is for that house and send them a note. Send them a letter and ask if they are interested in selling the house.

If you happen to have investors who are investors that want to buy properties in a particular area, this is your opportunity to reach out to anyone out in that area and find out if they're interested in selling their house. You may have investors that are looking to buy something. However if that house is not necessarily a perfect fit for your investor, you can still sell it for those people. Just look around you will see all kinds of things going on. You'll hear things with people that are looking to sell. Again, be sure when you're having those conversations that you let everybody know that you can help sell a property also. You can help navigate those waters so that those sellers are taken care of. Many times you'll get the 'for sale by owner' and they believe they really truly believe that they know everything. The for sale by owners tend to sell their homes for less money than a licensed real estate agent will sell it for on the market. It is important to listen to the conversations and ask the questions and you will find people out there ready to sell!

Garel Master's Class

Seller Appointments

Let's talk about seller appointments. You've talked to people. You've identified people that are interested in selling their house. Now we need to get them in for that appointment.

The best way really is just say, "Hey, how about I come by your house, take a look at it, talk with you guys about it and tell you what it's worth." They're interested in selling. They now need to know the numbers. and of course many have the thought process, "You know, 123 Main Street's my address - so what's my house worth on the market according to the comps?"

My answer is along the lines of:
"Without having seen your house, if 12345 happen, here's where the market says your house
should be listed at. I haven't seen your house. I don't know if that's the case. You could have updated bathrooms. You could have updated the kitchen. You could have updated the flooring. You could have added a room to it. You could have done all kinds of fabulous stuff to this house which makes it worth more than what the norm is, and the only way for me to know exactly what your house should be priced is to see it. So how about I stop by tomorrow at two o'clock and talk with you and your spouse? I'll take a look at the house and then let's talk about the pricing."

Garel Master's Class

So the best thing to do when you are getting those appointments is to say, "Let me come by and take a look at it. Show me around and then I'll have a better idea on the pricing."

This gives you that opportunity to go in, and do your research on what stuff is selling in the neighborhood. This gives you the opportunity when you go in for that appointment. You are going to bring a whole packet with your listing presentation that includes pictures of homes that you feel are comparable to their home to show them. You can ask, "Does your house look like this house? Here are the pictures. What's different? Where do you feel your house should be priced at compared to this one?" This allows you to go in and actually physically see everything with your eyes. They love showing you the house and they're going to tell you when they did - updates and conversions. This is your opportune time! I walk in for that appointment. I set my stuff down on the table and I said let's go take a look at your house. I am not there to immediately sit down and start talking about the pricing, because all I've seen is a front door and the way to wherever I put my stuff down. I don't know the whole house. Go on a tour and look at the whole house. Walk around the house, go outside in the backyard, go outside in the front yard. You may choose to look at the neighborhood as you drive around. You may choose to drive around before your

Garel Master's Class

appointment to check out the neighborhood and the amenities and everything else to have an idea of what this neighborhood has to offer. These points give you a great talking point. Once you've talked with them about the house, ask them where they feel it should be priced at and then you guys start to talk about where it really should be priced based on what they're wanting and how long they would like it to sit on the market or what their motivation is. If they need to sell quickly, price it a little bit lower. If they want to get a higher price point (over price) for it maybe they're going to let it sit for a while. I'm still up in arms over that one-because you can price it right, put it under potential multiple offers and still get that higher price.

So have that conversation with them. Once you have that conversation with them, you've built the rapport. You have the trust. Then they're willing to sign that listing agreement with you.

Be sure when you're booking that appointment you do see the house so you really know what's in the house, what it looks like and how it and how it compares with the other homes that have sold and are on the market in the neighborhood. If you have the opportunity, you have a couple of days before that appointment book some appointments to go see the other stuff that is on the market in the neighborhood and go see it with your own eyes versus just the picture, because now you can say,

Garel Master's Class

"I've been in that house, I've been in that one, and I've looked at that one." It makes you the expert. So be sure to do your homework and get into the home to have that meeting so that you can get that listing agreement signed.

Garel Master's Class

Seller: Marketing Your Listing

Let's talk a little bit about marketing. You have a listing that you've worked hard for. You've had the conversations. You've identified a seller. You've gone on that appointment. They've signed the listing agreement. Wonderful, congratulations! Now, let's market! Marketing is not doing the three piece, put a sign in the yard, put it in the MLS and pray that it gets sold. Let's do more and be a better agent than that.

The first thing is you need to do is sit down with your seller, or maybe stand up and walk
around and point things out and let them know what needs to be cleaned up. This especially is the case if they're still living there.

What do we need to take down? What do we need to clean up? What do we need to put here? Maybe they can box a bunch of stuff up and get it ready for photos. They can put the boxes either in storage or in the garage. If it's vacant we want to make sure it's nice and clean.

Have things been done such as has it been painted? Has it been cleaned? I cannot stress how well a clean house will show! It doesn't have to have all the fancy bells and whistles. It doesn't have to have all the new things in there. If it's clean, it looks clean and smells clean. It makes a huge difference. People will see past

Garel Master's Class

all of the lack of updates and stuff and they can envision what they can do to this house. They don't like a dirty house. They don't like it to smell like dogs and cats. They don't want it to smell like that delicious laced with garlic and spices or the thing that you cooked last night. They don't want it to smell like some sort of aromatherapy. They don't want to smell heavy essential oils or fragrances. That stuff will actually turn people off.

So have those conversations about having very neutral clean smells. If you have clients that maybe don't want to listen to you about that or you feel there may be a little bit of a challenge on that, get somebody that is a Stager. You'll find somebody that'll come in and for a very low cost will come in and be the bad guy. They'll come in and give your client homework, and guess what? They're the professional Stager. They're the one that will give that homework list of things like: "Let's move the table over." "Let's clean up all of this stuff." "Over here, let's empty the bookshelf." "Let's take all this stuff down off of the wall." "We're going to need a fresh coat of paint." They'll come in and do all of that and when you have the professional come in and tell your clients about that, it makes you the hero too, because now you've spent some money to have somebody else come in and identify what needs to be done.

Once that house is ready for photos it is time to get a photographer out there. Please get a professional and don't take it on your telephone. Don't take it on your iPad. Don't come in and do the photos yourself unless

Garel Master's Class

you are a professional photographer and know what you're doing.

I have a nice camera. I have a really nice SLR camera. I am not the best at using it I will hire somebody to come in and take those photos and do what they do best because we can both take pictures side by side I can guarantee you whose photos look better: the photographers not mine. It makes a big difference to have somebody come in and know exactly what to do with the angles, the lighting and everything else.

Be sure to put in a good description in the MLS. Don't just say, "As is. For sale. Come see it! Make an offer."

Describe the house. Paint a picture in your description that you are going to put into the MLS for everybody to read. Be sure that when you do put it in the MLS if your clients are okay with it and have agreed on the listing agreement.

Syndicate that information out on the internet. It goes out to Zillow and realtor.com, Redfin and everywhere else. You want your description to go out there. I do not allow anybody to do the zestimate. I'm the one that's making the choice. My client and I are making that choice on the price. I don't need the computer making that choice for me and putting a number in somebody's head. I don't allow comments because you always have that bad seed that's going to come in and say something nasty that you're going to have to maintain and watch

Garel Master's Class

and either delete or make comments on. So I will put the listing out there where you can see it, you can see the description, you can see the price and you have my contact information. Once you have all of that set up be sure that you are also doing social media and marketing.

This is where you're going to go out. Before I even go live, I've got the photos, I've got everything ready. I'm going to click the button to take it live on a particular date, I will go out there beforehand and I will do a little video. Out here in Texas we are allowed to do 24 hours we can Market to the public 24 hours before it goes live. I will take my opportunity to do a Facebook live video, a small little video with some pictures to put on Instagram and elsewhere on social media like LinkedIn and all those places. Market that home pre-market like, "Hey guess what's coming tomorrow?! Tomorrow morning this house is going live. You're going to get a sneak peek of it right now!"

I really like to take houses live on a Thursday. Thursday is great because people see it. Friday they start to plan their weekend. Saturday and Sunday I will do a double open house so that I have all the public come out and see me. As soon as it goes live I've marketed it. Pre-marketing in my Facebook live video so that everybody knows to come see me at the open house that first weekend. Double open house Saturday and Sunday gets as much traffic through get as much

Garel Master's Class

interest. Early on is the time when things will hit, so I get all of that taken care of first thing.

Make sure that you're still continuing to do some social media. This is when I'm going to do a broker open house that first week after we've gone live. After that first weekend I'm going to have a broker open house. I'm going to invite a bunch of Agents over. I'm going to have questions that I would like them to answer. I want them to pop through and see the condition of the home. I ask them, "How do you feel its price is set? What do you think could improve it? Do you happen to have any clients that might be interested? What do you think about the area?" Pick out some questions and get some advice from other agents that are coming through and taking a look at the house. Here is a little trick where the Broker Open House helps:

If you have a challenging client who really insists on overpricing the house or maybe not fixing something that you've said really should be fixed to sell it, this is when those agents give you all that feedback and then you provide that feedback to your seller and then your seller realizes. that everybody's saying the same thing and maybe that's what they need to do.

Be sure that even throughout all of this you continue to market the property. Don't just stick the sign in there. Don't just do your marketing the first weekend and then give up. You market that property until you sell. This means if you can get multiple open houses, even

Garel Master's Class

afterwards if you can get other people through and ask them their opinion on what they've seen. Be sure you flag it on social media the minute you do something. If your client suddenly finished painting or did a new roof or something with whatever was, announce it on social media! For example: " This listing just got a new roof, go check it out!" "Great house with brand spanking new roof!"

Be sure that you continue to market your listing. I like some little Flyers. You can put some flyers in the kitchen. Talk to your Title Company about a property profile. They'll put together a book that you can actually leave on the counter that will have deed restrictions and all kinds of stuff for the neighborhood.

Leave it on the counter so that anybody coming through can flip through that and take a look at it. Next to that I will actually put a binder, and in that binder I'll have a copy of the survey. I'll have a copy of the seller's disclosure. I will have a copy of the listing so that you can see all of the information in there. When I talk to my clients I ask them to put together a spreadsheet for me or give me the invoices for everything that they've done on the houses.

I want to know when they did maintenance to the air conditioner. I want to know when was the last time they painted. I want to know when was the last time they updated the flooring. If they remodeled the kitchen I want to know when I want to know when they did all of

Garel Master's Class

those things and how much it cost. Put that in a spreadsheet. That sheet will be in that binder that I leave on the counter. Also, I leave a lot of information on the home so that at any given notice when somebody's walking through the house and they have some questions, they can flip through either one of those books and take a look and get some information on that home. It eliminates a lot of questions, so be sure you provide the stuff there.

Again I cannot stress enough: Do not stop marketing the house after the first weekend. Don't think "I'm done. I've got it. I did my open house -I'm done."

You're not done until that house is under contract, closes and your client has their money and you've made your commission.

Garel Master's Class

You are not done until that moment so continue to market that house. Continue to make phone calls around the neighborhood. Be sure you do the open houses. Be sure you do social media marketing. If you want to do a mailer, do a simple postcard mailer and mail it throughout the neighborhood. If you're able to do door knocking in that neighborhood, please check on the community and the city criteria. We have some cities around here close to the Austin area that require permits before you can door knock. Follow those rules and regulations, however door knock. I love a door knock before an open house and I will give a flier to anybody that answers the door and invite them to the open house.

I want them to come see it. I might say, "Hey, if you have anybody else that you know that might be wanting to move into the area, invite them over to the open house to come check it out!"

Most of the neighbors don't mind when you door knock and invite because I'm not asking for anything else other than "Come check it out! You've got to see what they did to the house -it's really great!"

So, be sure you continue to talk about the house. You talk to the neighbors, you talk to everybody else. You mark it on social media. You have the MLS. You do everything that you can. This is not a one and done stick the sign out there, put it in the MLS and done.

Garel Master's Class

Again, you are not done until that house closes and your client has the money and you have a major commission. Now, go out there and market a house!

Garel Master's Class

Seller: Receive Offers

You have a seller and you've just received an offer or maybe you've received multiple offers for that seller's listing. Let's talk about first just a single offer, You received an offer and it either came in your inbox the agent called you. There are multiple ways that you can receive it. It could have been an email with just the terms on it and the agent is telling you that they're going to get you the signed offers coming soon. They could have just thrown iit in the email and sent you the signoff or didn't even call you. Maybe they did a combination.

Great, you have that offer! The first thing you want to do is acknowledge with the agent that you have received the offer if they call. Let's say they sent you the terms in an email. Take a look at it, they're getting ready to send you the signed offer. Take a look at the email right then and there while you have them on the phone.

Say, "I see it." If you have any questions about what they sent, ask at that point. Then if they just sent you an email, reply back to the email. I would also recommend giving the agent a call and letting them know that you did receive the offer and you were looking at it. You should already have an agreement with your seller when they would like to look at the offers because if they're working they're not going to want to look in the middle of the day - especially if they're busy or if they're out on vacation on a business trip or something like that. You're going to have a time that they're going to want to review

Garel Master's Class

things so you will let your seller know that you have received an offer, and at that time that you guys have agreed upon you will talk with them about the offer. At this moment you are going to run through it and identify the details so that you can talk with them about it.

Many Agents will just forward that offer over to their sellers. I don't. Reason being it's a lot of legal jargon and most of the people out there are not going to truly understand what it says.

They see a comment in there on that contract on that offer contract that says house being sold as is and they automatically think well that means that even if they do an inspection too bad so sad! I'm not going to do anything they're paying for this house as is regardless. In the state of Texas you still have that option period and that is a second negotiation if your inspector finds something that wasn't identified before. A lot of times the sellers do not truly understand the verbiage in those documents.

Instead what I will do is put together a list. Whether it's a spreadsheet, because my clients like spreadsheets - whether it's something that I put together in a simple email, I will also include a net sheet. You can get those really pretty snazzy net sheets from your Title Company. They'll actually put one together for you can send them the offer! They'll put it all together for you and it's very nice so it shows what your client will net at the end.

Garel Master's Class

I will go through that offer and I will look at the details. How much are they offering? How much are they going to be putting as a down payment? What kind of loan are they doing? Is it a cash deal? When are they wanting to close? What does earnest look like? What does the option period look like? How many days? How much money are they putting down for option? Are they asking for a home warranty? What about the survey?? What about if it's in an HOA? How much are they planning to pay for the HOA transfer and all of the other stuff that goes along with it?

I am looking at all of those details and I'm identifying those details and I'm taking note of those details so that I can run through those details with my client. In addition, as I've looked through that offer and I've had a chance to talk to the agent, most of the time you'll have a chance to talk to the agent. There are some that will not answer the phone and will not talk to you.

I like talking to them because I am going to feel out their client by talking to the agent. I'm going to find out their motivation. I'm going to find out how qualified they are. I'm going to find out all of that. In addition in that offer if the agent did not send me a pre-approval or a pre-qualification letter or or a statement that shows that they have the cash if they're paying cash for the house I'm going to call and get that because I want to talk to the lender, and I want to ask the lender of series of questions. I want to know how qualified these clients are. Can you meet the close date? They said they want

Garel Master's Class

to close in 20 days. Where are they in the process that you can guarantee that you can close in 20 days? So there's various different things and I'm going to do my due diligence before I give all the details to my client.

Next, I'll talk to my client about that and because I have talked to the lender, I've talked to the agent, I've read through the offer and I have an idea of how that offer feels too. I'm going to let him know the lender was really super easy to reach in fact the lender called me before I had a chance to call the lender this lender I feel like this lender is going to be a great lender to work with or maybe I've worked with that lender before and I have some history: this is a great Bank this is a great lender I've worked with this actual lender or lending officer directly before. I've worked with this agent before and this agent was very communicative with me.

If you can't reach the agent, you can't reach the lender. Talk to your client letting them know that the terms in this offer don't look so great. You might say, "Understand if you decide to take this offer we may have to push closing because I have been having a hard time reaching anybody in regards to this offer and I want to prepare you for the worst case scenario."

If everything is smooth, everybody's communicating with me, everybody's talking, then they're providing me with what I need. If everybody's been wonderful on this then I've been able to reach them really easily. The agent tells me that if I just send her a text message she'll give

Garel Master's Class

me a call back. If she happens to be in with another client she'll call me back as soon as she can. I've been able to talk to the lender and gotten a lot of information. The lender gave me his cell phone number. This one looks like we will be able to communicate well and this lender says he's never missed a close date, in fact he usually can push up the close date by a few because these clients are already in underwriting.

That information helps you determine how that transaction is going to look so that you can prepare your clients because what you don't want to happen is you haven't been able to reach anybody. You can't reach the lender and your client decides to take the offer and you don't prepare them for there's a possibility that this closing may be pushed because some things on here look a little funny. If you haven't been able to reach anybody but closing gets pushed or these buyers pull out a week before closing because say they don't end up not qualifying for the loan, and if you didn't talk to the lender you really didn't know that and they still have that right to pull out because they didn't they couldn't get the loan. Then what your client's going to be really upset with you and you didn't do a great job to prepare them for what was actually coming.

So be sure you talk to all parties. Communication is essential, it's not essential just at the beginning, it is essential all the way to the end.

Garel Master's Class

Now when you get to closing, say the scenario is that you get multiple offers. Happy day! We like that because this is where you can push that offer price up, or in a slow Market you push that offer price to list price so your client can get what they're looking for - possibly more multiple offers. Same thing, contact everybody and say, "Thank you for sending me the offer I have received. I have received multiple offers and I will be reviewing everything at whatever time." If you have multiple offers I really like to encourage you to contact everybody that has put an offer in give them a deadline or highest and best give that agent the opportunity to talk to their clients and come back with what they feel is highest and best.

Those buyers want the house and they will be very upset if they learn after the fact that there were multiple offers and they could have come up with ten thousand more to maybe win the deal and they didn't even get the opportunity.

It's in your best interest for your clients to solicit the highest and best and it's in the best interest for the buyer's agent to be able to go back to their buyers and say, "Hey that house that you guys love they got four offers on that plus yours they have five offers in hand the agent said that they're going to take highest and best by tomorrow at noon. Where do you guys want to be? How much do you guys love this house?" That gives those buyers an opportunity to potentially win that house by bringing up their offer and changing their terms.

Garel Master's Class

Give them the courtesy of that and you can have some conversations too because the agent should be asking you what your clients want.

This is when you can say, "My clients want a quick close." "My clients want a lease back." "My clients would like the buyers to pay for the title policy." You can tell them some of those things. Your clients will tell you what is okay to talk about and those are the things that you can help get into those contracts and if everything else works well for those buyers, they have that potential to win the deal.

Remember wherever you're at depending on what the rules are as far as offer price in Texas we cannot disclose that I can tell you that my clients want a lease back and they want a quick close and they don't want to pay for the title policy and they don't have a survey and they they're saying the buyer needs to pay for a new survey.

If asked, you might reply, "I can't tell you what the highest offer I received is that's confidential private information so instead I will talk about the terms that I can talk about." If your client gives permission, you can talk about dollars. You have to get that permission from your seller to make sure what you can and cannot talk about the multiple offers.

Create a spreadsheet create a spreadsheet with all of those same details that we had talked about before with

Garel Master's Class

the offer price, the down payment, what kind of loan, earnest money, option period, option money - all of the details put that together in a spreadsheet. Then do a side-by-side comparison with all of the offers.

In the bottom you're going to have some notes like "Lender was very easy to talk with" or "Lender called me in advance and gave me all the information." These clients are already in underwriting they can technically close in two weeks if we want a two-week close whatever the case is so that you can actually provide that spreadsheet to your clients and they can see a side-by-side comparison with your comments and this is something you guys will talk about this will help your clients make make a judgment call on which offer they want to go with.

I also want to mention that once they have decided on which buyer they want to work with they can still negotiate that contract. So, if they've chosen buyer a because the terms are really great and everything's good but they'd like to see a little bit more money because buyer C came in with more money but the terms were not so great, and they didn't like the lender - or maybe there was no no lender letter provided or whatever the case is they like - they can go back and say, "Hey, we want to work with you guys if you bring the price up."

Garel Master's Class

You can select that way too and pick one that you're going to work with and then ask them to bring up the price to win the deal and still have the negotiations.

Negotiations go on until the last party signs and that contract is executed. Therefore, if you like a buyer, go back and say, "We like everything… we just need this one thing changed and once we get that changed we're a done deal." Take a look at all of the different things be sure you communicate with everyone be sure you look at the details and provide your client with the details this will help you and your client communicate with each other understand what's going on and identify what's best when they receive an offer so go out there get that listing and get some offers in!

Garel Master's Class

Seller: Negotiate the Deal

You've got your house for sale and the buyers come in. You're gonna get buyers. You're going to get all kinds of offers coming through. Depending on the market that you're in, you can have a couple of offers come through at first. Early on those tend to be the investor offers. Those are the ones that are your "discount- buy it super cheap -put a little bit of lipstick on it and then turn around and sell it for $200,000 more than they paid for it."

They are looking for a super super super cheap deal. They're going to come in $200,000 below what you've listed it at, hoping that you'll take it because they'll close in seven days with cash. Talk to your sellers in advance so that they know there's a possibility that you're going to get some of those offers in. Let them know not to be offended. They send those offers in all the time. They don't even reach back out to see if I got the offer and what happened because they throw hundreds of them out every day. They are just writing them up left and right hoping that something will stick.

You're gonna get phone calls from the other agents just like I described on the buyer's side.

These are things that you want to hear. You're going to ask questions when that offer comes through from that buyer's agent. Tell them, "I Need a lender letter. I need a pre-qualification, a pre-approval." I need to see that because I'm going to call the lender and I'm going to ask the lender a variety of questions depending on what the Market's like. I'm going to ask the questions about how qualified their clients are. I'm going to ask a variety of different questions to the lender on the buyers and I'm going to get some information. I'm going to get a feel if I can't reach that lender. I've left the lender a message and the lender does not call me back, doesn't text me back and I can't get anybody to talk to me, I'm going to have a hard time reaching that lender during this transaction. Guess what? If the buyers don't qualify for a loan, this deal doesn't close and we've pulled it off the market for naught. So I need to be able to communicate with that lender. I'll make that phone call in advance before I've even had a chance to talk to them because then I can ask him the questions. I'm going to take a look at that offer. I'm going to go through it. I'm going to bullet point various aspects of the offer price like how much money are they putting as their down payment and what does that loan look like. Why? Because if they come in they've got a $450,000 offer and they're putting two hundred thousand dollars down as a down payment, that tells me a little something about these buyers.

They're financially savvy.

Garel Master's Class

If they have two hundred thousand dollars to put down and they're only taken out a $250,000 loan, that's pretty impressive. They look pretty well qualified to me.

I'm gonna look what are they asking for, how much they put down for option money, (typically 0.1 percent of the offer price) and at a $450,000 offer price I'm expecting about four hundred dollars for option money because that's the ability to take the house off the market for the buyers to walk away for any reason. Then my clients get to keep that money so it needs to be worth the while of taking it off the market. A lot of these new agents are coming in and being like, "I just put a hundred dollars down for the option period and let's ask for 10 days." No, for a $450,000 house offer price you're gonna come in with at least four hundred dollars. I will negotiate that up to four hundred dollars if you want that 10 days. So make it worth the while. A hundred dollars is not worth keeping it off the market for 10 days. If you want one day for a hundred dollars, sure, but not for 10 days.

Earnest money that's the money that you're keeping over there at the Title Company is kind of your depository money. It is saying "Yes I do want the house." That's your layaway money. Think of those layaway plans. You're putting the house on layaway and so you're putting down your layaway deposit typically one percent. To me, money is important. It's not as important to me as the option money though because the option money pulls

Garel Master's Class

the house off the market. If the buyers walk away what do my sellers get to pocket? So for a $450,000 house, I'm expecting four thousand forty five hundred dollars for earnest money give or take. This could be a little bit lower could be higher. I know a lot of Agents think that if you put a heavy amount of earnest money down that looks better. Actually that is not true because if they back out during the option period they get to take that earnest money with them. How does that benefit my sellers?

It doesn't. I like more option money.

What are the buyers asking for? Are they asking for a home warranty? Are they asking for the sellers to pay for the title policy? Are they asking the sellers to pay for a new survey? If there's an HOA, how much are the buyers willing to pay to obtain those HOA documents and do the transfer? If they're putting down that they're only willing to pay a hundred dollars, then my client is going to be out of pocket for four five six seven hundred dollars. If the buyers put down that there's more money they're willing to pay four hundred dollars to get HOA documents and do the transfer, and all of that seems a little bit more equivalent. So I'm looking at these various points. I am going through that contract with the fine-tooth comb and identifying the different items in there and I'm listing those out. Then I'm going to talk to my client.

Garel Master's Class

Before that you can reach out to your title rep also and get a net sheet. Send in the contractor they'll put a net sheet together! That'll be a beautiful, pretty net sheet that will total an estimate your client will walk away with at closing - and that's what they really want to see. Your client wants to see that final number.

Therefore do all you can and provide all of that for your clients so they can see those numbers and they can make those decisions. Because as you get that, again, it's not hard set in stone until everybody has signed and it's been executed and then the buyers have sent money option and earnest money over the Title company who has then received everything. Before then it's still all part of negotiations and you can negotiate based on any of that. If you don't like that your client says, "I don't want to pay for the survey. We have one." Let the buyer's agent know. Cross that out. You can make changes to that. I like to have a conversation with the agent and say, "Send me over a clean contract," or I'll make the changes on the existing one. We'll initial it and they can initial next to the changes. Be sure that even when you're negotiating the contract that both the buyer and the seller side are a win-win situation.

You want to make people feel comfortable, especially at this part of the transaction. It's the beginning and if you guys can't make this a win-win at this point, the

Garel Master's Class

transaction is going to be tough and will probably fall apart and unravel later on. So be sure to take a look at all the parts, ask the questions, talk to all parties to make sure you know exactly what to do, where to go and how to proceed.

Garel Master's Class

Leases

Why Lease?

Leases are something that not a lot of Agents do. They don't want to spend the time on a lease because they feel that the money's not there. Leases are a great opportunity for all agents -especially the newer agents- for some on-the-job training! Working with clients, showing homes, finding homes, and negotiating some deals. Believe it or not, yes you do negotiate some things in a lease and you will get a paycheck at the end of it. Why would you turn that down? You get on the job experience and a paycheck… can't beat that!

Leases give you on the job experience and a paycheck!

When other agents are turning these transactions down, take them! Leasing clients are happy to work with an

Garel Master's Class

agent because a lot of the agents will turn them down. When they discover the challenges of finding some of the leases, and when they discover that some of the negotiations are a little bit harder, they are happy to have representation to fight for them!

Okay, so we know that we get on-the-job training and a paycheck. It's beautiful. What else about a lease client and a lease transaction is beautiful? Their lease eventually ends. When it ends, guess what? If you've had the conversation *[we will talk about "the conversation" in a few chapters!]* with them while you are helping them find the lease, and they work on credit saving money, and you stay in touch with them, those lease clients become buyers! Oh, did I mention they also know people. If you've done a great job for them, they will refer you to all of their friends and family and anybody they can. Now your database is growing because you have a cheerleader.

On the job training
   ..A paycheck
     ..Future Buyer
        ..Growing your database and business

Take the time. Learn it. Work it. Put some money in your pocket.

Garel Master's Class

What To Expect When Applying for a Property Lease

Are you prepared to pay double rent? Typically, a property will be held a maximum of 2 weeks from the acceptance of the applicant. Do not expect the agent/owner to hold the property longer even though some occasionally do.

Please be advised that each company, that qualifies prospective tenants, has their own criteria; however, typically they will require the following:

- Each person over the age of 18 years must complete a separate application. The application form is at the discretion of each company.
- Application fees, payable to the listing agent/agency, vary and are NON-REFUNDABLE.
- Credit check- the higher the score the better. Some companies may accept a low credit score with extra security deposit or a guarantor.
- Residential history check- a good history with landlords.
- Income- the applicant must make 3 times (gross) the amount of rent. Some companies require more than just 1 adult to make this amount. Pay stubs or proof of income must be provided.
- Criminal history check.
- There may be an administration fee
- A copy of a drivers' license or some form of

Garel Master's Class

identification.

o A security deposit, payable to the owner/landlord, is typically required to hold the property and will not be refunded once the applicant(s) have been accepted.

Be prepared to have the first month's rent and pet deposit, if applicable, ready at time of signing the lease and receiving keys.

REMEMBER: Each company has their own criteria which must be adhered to if you want to lease their property.

Garel Master's Class

Leasing: Finding & Showing homes; Overcoming Challenges

Before you take clients out to go look at homes for a lease, be sure you've had "the conversation!"

Leasing is not strictly black and white on how things are done. Leasing has many shades of in between. So before you take clients out to go look at homes for a lease, be sure you've had "the conversation" What do I mean by "the conversation?"

I mean is this: find out the motivation of your clients. Find out anything in their background that could affect their lease. This is when you have to be very blunt with your clients. You need to find out if they have past evictions. Let them know there will be a background check and a credit check. They will check jobs and rental history. They will look to see if the clients are making 3x the cost of rent. This is the time for your client to come clean with you.

Tell them, "I need to know do you guys have poor credit scores? Any evictions under your belt? Any sort of criminal record?"

Once I have that information about what's going on with my clients, then I have the ability to talk with landlords, with owners, with property management companies,

Garel Master's Class

and with other leasing agents to find out if a property that I plan to show my client is a potential for them.

What I mean by that is if their background or credit score disqualifies them for a property they love and they're expecting me to get them this house now, but discover they are not qualified and their application fee was wasted, who are they going to be mad at?

Sure, they're mad at the landlord for not taking them because they feel like they should be taken, however, they're really going to be mad at me because I didn't do my job. I didn't do what was needed to make sure that they qualified for this house.

Remember, before you take anybody out to go look at the property, ask those questions. Have the conversation. If that isn't enough, there is another reason to have these conversations.

Once I know their obstacles, then I know how to work through those challenges! Everybody has something going on. Even if they have stellar credit scores and great jobs. It may be that they've only been in their job for a year and a half and the landlord's looking for at least a two-year minimum on the job. There are things we can do! I can get a letter from the company. We could get a letter from the boss saying that this person is awesome and they're up for a promotion come at the

Garel Master's Class

end of the year. If they've had an eviction and that was say five years ago, we could get a note from current landlords saying they've been stellar clients and they've paid on time as well as taken care of the place. The landlord can say that they would rent to them again. If they have a poor credit score and I discover they recently went through a divorce,

I now have talking features because when you go through a divorce your credit gets screwed up.

I now have my own great conversations that I can use to overcome the landlord or property management company objections.

This is why you need to know their background.

Once you know the obstacles, you can find solutions to the challenges!

Garel Master's Class

Once you have the background, and a list of homes that meet what your clients are looking for, then you're going to want to make those phone calls. Make the phone calls to whoever's in charge of doing the applications: the leasing agent, the landlord, the property management company, and talk with them. They have criteria. Again, have the conversation. Just because it's written there in black and white on their sheet does not mean that they will not be willing to work with you. I've done that. You can relay their story to the landlord. For instance, "My client recently went through a divorce and it really messed up her credit score. She's got a great job. She's got money saved up and she's working on getting everything back in order. This one little setback kind of messed things up and she really needs to get into a lease right now. She has the money right now to get in. Would this be something that you would consider taking?"

If they say "no", thank them and move on to the next one. However, if they say, "Tell me more.."
Then tell them a little bit more. Have that conversation. You're providing in enough information
to get them interested so that you can get the deal done. We don't have to give them everything- we just need to give them enough to make them like your clients and want to lease to your clients.

Garel Master's Class

Lastly, be sure you communicate clearly with your clients because they need to know that the home they are looking at right now, the landlord said that they would take your application - however they want an additional three hundred dollars for a security deposit. Find out if they are okay with the work arounds the landlord needs. Get out there, ask those questions and get those people into a lease!

Garel Master's Class

Leasing Client Approved: Now What?

Your people have given you all their closet secrets. You know all of the skeletons. You know them by name. You've talked with property owners, leasing agents and property management companies. You've found out how you can get your clients the home that they love. Your clients have submitted the application and you've had that talk about the applications and the non-refundable fees on those applications. Now you get either the call, or your clients get an email or a call that says they've been approved! Now what?

Depending on how the paperwork was filled out, now it's time to take a look at when they want money submitted. I really recommend that you have another conversation with the person in charge again - the leasing agent, the landlord, the property management company -and have another conversation with them and ask if they would like them to go ahead and submit the security deposit now. If so, who should that be made out to? Do they want that done electronically or would a personal check be okay? Does it need to be a cashiers or a money order? Ask them if your clients should pay the prorated amount of the rent now or should they pay the first full month's rent? Who should that be made out to? Automatic deposit or personal check?

You need to have that information because your clients are going to come back to, and will be thinking about getting the keys, not about writing the checks. So be sure you find out how all of that works. Each home it's going to work differently. For example, some may want the security deposit now, some within 72 hours, some in 24 hours etc. They may decide to have the prorated rents paid first and then continue on. Find out how their system works and how they want things done. Now you have the conversation with your client and walk them through that whole process as you explain what is going on. It is very, very important that you have all of that done and make sure everybody understands.

Your job doesn't finish when they get accepted. It finishes when you get paid, and I recommend that even after you've gotten paid, your job is not truly done because those leasing clients become buyers.

Those leasing clients know referrals. So once you find out exactly how everything needs to be, let your clients know so that you can do some things to help them: maybe that means maybe help coordinating with them to get the checks over to the other parties. Help do what you need to do. Once you've got that all taken care of, there's something else that you want to think about: there's usually that inventory and condition form and that's often submitted within the first three to five days of moving in. Oftentimes the other side will not give this form to your clients. I will actually print it and hand it to my clients and explain to them how to do it. I'll encourage them that once they've completed it to send it back to me and I'll send it over to the agent. Why?

Garel Master's Class

Because now I also have a hard copy so that when they're ready to move out if there's any sort of dispute I can help and I'm right in there with them! Once your clients are all taken care of and they've got keys and made the payments that have been requested, don't forget to get yourself paid! This is where you create an invoice. Maybe your brokerage has an invoice template that they use that you can use. Send that over along with your W-9.

If you're an independent and not part of a brokerage, then you're your own broker and you'll have your own broker's W-9. If you're part of another Market Center, another brokerage, then they should have a W-9 that you can use. Send both of those documents over to the other Leasing Agent, Property Management Company or the Landlord so they will be able to send you a payment.

Again, leasing there is no black and white but a lot of gray, so that payment can happen really quickly. I've submitted documents on a Tuesday and I had them say they pay out on Thursday and by Friday I had a check! However, I've had some where the communication skills on their end were not so stellar and was still waiting on a check after two months! So, the best recipe for leasing is: keep your paperwork straight, and your clients happy.

Garel Master's Class

Submitting an Application for a Lease

You will have clients that come around and they see houses they love and they want to just submit applications left and right. What they don't realize, (and I hope that you *do* realize) is that those application fees are non-refundable.

Anybody that is 18 or older that will be living in that home must complete an application and submit an application fee. Sometimes there's even an administration fee that they throw in there to make a little extra money.

Therefore, if an application is a hundred dollars per person and you have three people in the house that are 18 or older, that's three hundred dollars just to see if you can get that house.

If they're doing that four times, that's twelve hundred dollars right off the bat. They are paying the amount of a monthly mortgage payment.

Garel Master's Class

Do your clients really want to spend that much money hoping that that application is accepted?

Do your due diligence and have the conversations you need to have and talk about any kind of challenges that your client might have and how do you overcome them *before* submitting that application. Find out if they will even accept them. For example, if the landlord said that they require a minimum of a 680 credit score, and your client has a 670, don't submit the application. They won't get that house.

Applications come in all shapes and sizes so know whether or not this is an application that you will download and have your clients fill out, or is this an application that they will provide whether they provide a hard copy of. Most will provide you a link.

Again, once an application is submitted, the money is non-refundable, so you want to make sure that this is a house your clients love, <u>and</u> that they can get into this house. Do your due diligence, communicate and be their superhero.

Garel Master's Class

Open Houses

Tips for a Successful Open House

Productivity Coach Donna Garel's

Top 5 tips for a Successful Open House

1. Before you get there: brush up on the details of the house so you go in prepared. Print out the MLS details and have a list of other homes in the area and their stats in case questions arise. This gives you expertise on the neighborhood.

2. Get there early to set up. Make sure you have forms to get contact information and the house looks spic and span. Make sure it is well lit and the blinds are open.

3. **Timing, Timing, Timing!** Those living in a metro area should host their open houses from 11:00 a.m. to 3:00 p.m. If you're out in the suburbs, host your open house between 12:00 p.m. to 4:00 p.m.

4. Make sure you advertise your Open House on social media: Facebook, Instagram, Twitter, Blog, Realtor.com etc.

5. Use LOTS of signs to direct people to your open house and make sure the signs are a generous size. Size matters! Quantity does too!

Garel Master's Class

Navigating the Open House Contract

The ideal situation is a guest walking into your open house not having an agent, being familiar with contracts and wanting to put an offer in. If this is your listing, awesome you don't have to pay out a buyer's agent to earn the whole commission. If you are doing an open house for somebody else you can actually let them know that it's not your listing so you are going to go ahead and represent them since they're here with me and they can fill out the paperwork. It really just kind of depends on how that works right.

I always keep an accordion folder with me. It's in the car in my Realtor Box in the trunk. It always goes with me when I do an open house. In this folder you will see blank contracts.

All the most common blank contracts: we've got buyer representation documents, we have resale and new construction contracts, and, depending on the type of home it is we can get those filled out so that when somebody pops in and wants to put an offer on a house right then and there I know exactly how to run that! We can get the documents pulled out and filled out on the spot. Be sure you're prepared. You never know when that's going to happen to you and you don't want to not be prepared.

Garel Master's Class

If they want to put an offer on the house you don't have any documents with you and then they leave, they will go find somebody else and they will write the documents up and you have missed that opportunity. Do not miss an opportunity to be prepared!

Garel Master's Class

Open House note for Buyers and Sellers

I love putting a listing live on Thursday. Reason being, Thursday is really close to the weekend. I get it live on Thursday and advertise that open house over the weekend. That's when agents buyers agents are starting to comb the MLS. Buyers are starting to comb the internet to find those new properties that hit the market. They're looking for open houses for the weekend so that they can plan. They're planning around their schedule and seeing what's available - especially if they're going to want to purchase something soon.

Possibly they're just looking in their neighborhood. People are always looking right before the weekend, so if you market on Thursday, then you start to hit those lists. They're going to go looking on Saturday and Sunday.

If an agent doesn't look on Thursday, then Friday morning they're looking. Again, list on Thursday. I will actually hold open my own listings on Saturday and Sunday. This is something I do for my sellers. I want my sellers to know that I am working for them. When they see that I'm going out to do the open houses they get very excited and know that I am again working for them. I will actually go out to the house before my open house and the seller may be there and I will go and do a quick video about the home showing a few features

Garel Master's Class

enticing the audience and then posting that on social media and advertising for that open house to come! I love doing that when the seller's still there because they know that I'm doing extra marketing for them. So be sure to work that open house Saturday and Sunday. If you don't do it personally, make sure somebody does. It's really, really important when you first hit the market that first weekend. You draw a lot of attention to that house. The longer it sits on the market it starts to get stale. Therefore, draw as much interest and as many people as you can to come by that weekend.

Buyer's agents, you're looking for an open house. If you're farming your neighborhood and you see that brokerage XYZ down the street which is not yours has a house for sale, call that agent on the sign and ask if you can hold that house open! They should allow you to hold that house open if they're interested in selling it. I have agents call me all the time wanting to do open houses at my properties even if they're not at my brokerage and I'm okay with that if I'm not doing it and I don't have anybody else doing it. I'm happy for them too because I want again the advertising, and I understand that they're working to get leads off of that.

They're looking for the buyer leads, and who knows they may bring a buyer to me for that house. My goal is to sell it. So most agents will not mind if you ask if you can hold one of their listings open. Don't be scared to ask,

Garel Master's Class

because again, you're advertising for them for free. Another tip, in Texas, if you are holding a house open for another agent they should not charge you to do that. There should be no fee. You get to go in, you do the open house and the leads should be yours. Also you should not be required to turn over your list of contacts and guests to that other agent. If that agent is asking for that information from you -run!

Go do another house, because they're wanting you to work for free and give them that information. I'm not ready to share that information if I worked at the open house, so be sure you protect yourself.

I have seen it happen in the past and it shouldn't. I never ask for a list I just did. Anybody can come in that was interested in putting in an offer and if so was there another agent involved or are they going to bring me an offer I don't need your list of who came in and phone numbers and contact information. I'm expecting you to reach out and get those people as clients. So be sure that you protect yourself on that aspect and understand open houses are a great way to get leads.

I have received sellers and buyers from open houses and it's just a matter of working them, making sure that you make the guests comfortable when they come in. You always talk about hosting an open house and you're hosting it but you're working that open house, don't play

Garel Master's Class

Hostess where you do not gather information and do not find motivation and you do not reach back out to the clients. Be sure you work it, that's how you will get those leads and then when you are done with your open house be sure that with all the information that you've gathered in your open house book you reach back out to them. Phone calls, text message, or email. If you have an address, send them a note card. When you have down time at the open house, write out little note cards to anybody that's already been there. The reason that I like that book is because I can put some notes in there on each one of the clients and flip the page. Those notes are what I put in that note card.

I had one couple that came in with a little boy who had a cape on and he played Superman. What do you think my note card said? "Thank you so much for coming in. I really enjoyed having Superman check out the house!" It's something that's memorable that will remember you and if they choose to purchase and don't have an agent they will remember you and they will call you. So make it personal. Go out there and get some open houses!

Garel Master's Class

Prologue

I believe in our mission as Agents to help people achieve their goals while achieving ours, and I believe in you! My heart is to support individual Agents, Coaching Programs and Brokerages with empowering information and tools for success.

If this book was helpful to you and you are interested in more, you can check out my online Master's Program with this information and more sections including: Mastering Your Mindset, Fear of Failure, When to Fire a Client *(Yes! Sometimes we need to and we need to know when!)*, being aware of and using your inner voice and when not to take a client. It also has modules on overcoming thoughts like, "I'm being judged" or "I'm bothering someone" as well as conquering the fear of hearing "No".

Best of all, you can go through this class at your own pace, on your own team from your very own office.

Check out https://donnagarel.com/the-masters-program for more information.

www.ingramcontent.com/pod-product-compliance
Lightning Source LLC
Chambersburg PA
CBHW072216170526
45158CB00002BA/618